THE VIBE MANAGER

THE VIBE MANAGER

INSIDE THE CENTRAL COAST MARINERS
2023 A-LEAGUE CHAMPIONSHIP

ANDY BERNAL

FAIRPLAY
PUBLISHING

First published in 2023 by Fair Play Publishing

PO Box 4101, Balgowlah Heights, NSW 2093, Australia

www.fairplaypublishing.com.au

ISBN: 978-1-925914-90-0

ISBN: 978-1-925914-91-4 (ePub)

© Andy Bernal 2023

The moral rights of the author have been asserted.

All rights reserved. Except as permitted under the Australian Copyright Act 1968 (for example, a fair dealing for the purposes of study, research, criticism or review), no part of this book may be reproduced, stored in a retrieval system, communicated or transmitted in any form or by any means without prior written permission from the Publisher.

Cover design and typesetting by Leslie Priestley.

Front cover photograph of Andy Bernal with the A-League trophy at Umina Beach, July 2023. (Photo: Hayley O'Brien)

Back cover photograph of Andy Bernal and Jaynie Wignall Bernal at CommBank Stadium after Central Coast Mariners' Grand Final win, June 2023.

Photographs from the personal collection of Andy Bernal or supplied by Central Coast Mariners A-League club.

All inquiries should be made to the Publisher via hello@fairplaypublishing.com.au

A catalogue record of this book is available from the National Library of Australia.

DEDICATION

IN THE PAST FEW YEARS, NICK MONTGOMERY AND I HAVE lost a parent, special souls who were always by our side on our respective football journeys. We both wished they could have been with us in person on Grand Final day. It wasn't to be, but I know they were right there with us at CommBank Stadium on such a magnificent football occasion, forever shining bright from above and smiling down upon us.

This book is dedicated to Monty's mother, Candy Montgomery, and my father, Andres Bernal.

CONTENTS

Prologue: **23**	1
Foreword	3
Chapter 1: **Destiny Is Written**	5
Chapter 2: **Dead and Gone**	14
Chapter 3: **Return to Sender**	28
Chapter 4: **The Cup**	36
Chapter 5: **Windows and Closets**	40
Chapter 6: **Let's Ride**	46
Chapter 7: **Brick Walls and Coconuts**	56
Chapter 8: **Pictures Paint a Thousand Words**	60
Chapter 9: **I'm the Joker**	73
Chapter 10: **Aftermath**	80
Chapter 11: **The Big Dance**	85
Special Mentions	100
About Andy Bernal	102
Appendix: **Central Coast Mariners – The Road to the 2023 A-League Men Championship**	104

Compiled by Andrew Howe

PROLOGUE

23

I HAVE LED AN UNBELIEVABLE AND AMAZING LIFE. GUIDED
and maybe protected at times from above. I've had many firsts, including being the first Australian to play in Spain, the first Australian to captain an English football club and the first Canberra-born footballer to play for the Socceroos.

After many years in the wilderness, I returned to professional football in an athletic development, coaching and mentoring capacity, winning the 2023 A-League Championship in my first year. That achievement made me wonder if our destiny is written by a higher power. Was the number 23 the source of divine intervention? After all, it was 2023 when the Mariners became champions, it had been 23 years since I had retired from professional football, 23 years since I became a sports agent with SFX Sports Group, and 23 was David Beckham's jersey number at Real Madrid when I was his personal manager. Our company SFX also represented the great Michael Jordan at the time he first wore the 23 singlet. A coincidence maybe, but there were so many! And speaking of higher powers, the 23rd verse of the 23rd Psalm in the Bible provides reassurance of God's protection and guidance.

Unbelievably, the numbers 2 and 3 also tell the story of our Grand Final: 2 x 3 = 6, the number of goals we scored. And the difference between 2 and 3 is 1, the solitary goal that Melbourne City scored in the match. Read into it or chop it up however you want, but the maths doesn't lie!

The night before the Grand Final all the players and staff were given a sealed envelope with a letter inside. It was from our friend and Central Coast Mariners' Mindset Coach, Ezio Mormile. I was so moved by it, I have made it the book's foreword, word for word.

FOREWORD

TO MY DEAR AMIGO ANDY BERNAL, THE ORIGINAL WIZARD of Oz, and *Mr. Riding Shotgun*.

Being Grand Final week, I thought I would write a letter to each of the players and staff. Whatever happens I want you to know it is a privilege to call you a friend, amigo and workmate. From when I started reading your book, I could tell you were very intelligent and had a lot of courage. Indeed, in your book on page 9 you write "my parents passed on DNA that in many ways mirrored their own courage, strength, fortitude and willingness to live life as a wonderful adventure". Amigo, you live that every day!

"WHO WILL JUMP IN FIRST?"

I don't watch much soccer, but I love and study human behaviour and team dynamics. That moment in Canberra when you jumped in the pool first, I immediately knew that was a defining moment and pivotal moment in the season! That's why I keep going on about it.

It's not just that, it's the hours you spend with the boys. The genuine CARE you have for them. Cummings is the classic example, you have a profound influence on him, the boys and staff. They respond to you because you also have CREDIBILITY—first Australian in Spain, first captain in England, at Real Madrid with Beckham, etc. You also have VULNERABILITY through the story in your book. You are HONEST and you are AUTHENTIC.

The story of the "rowing machine" is also relevant. Very important, you did very well with that and so many other things. And I have not even mentioned your work in Athletic Development, or charity organisations, Indigenous groups, the young Academy boys. You are an amazing man, Andy, and of course you make me laugh, with quotes like, "At 16 years old you don't need an agent, you need talent."

Amigo, your mum, Margaret, and dad, Andres, would be so proud of you! Whatever happens in the Grand Final, if I'm going to WAR, I want Andy Bernal on my side! Life is beautiful, because of people like you, Andy Bernal!

Your amigo, Ezio Mormile

29 May 2023

OPPORTUNITY IS NOWHERE

CHAPTER 1

DESTINY IS WRITTEN

IT'S A CRAZY WORLD WE LIVE IN, A MYRIAD OF MYSTERIOUS ways. Twenty years on from the life-changing phone call I received from Tony Stephens (who at the time was David Beckham's agent and one of my bosses at SFX Sports Group), another phone call came in, this time from an unknown person who would again change and impact my life in an amazing way. It was a blessing from above, arriving at a time when, to be quite honest, I was going nowhere and could feel darkness once again rearing its ugly head.

No caller ID, but for some reason I decided to answer it, interrupting another day of staring blankly into nowhere from the balcony of my Canberra apartment. Contemplating, thinking about thinking, somehow trying to figure out how I could one day re-enter the football workforce and the football community that had turned their backs on me, never to be forgiven for my sins of self-destruction. Answering the phone, I was preparing to hurl abuse at the cold caller, assuming it was just another human trying to screw me over in life, as if life itself had not finished its punishment with me yet.

I was surprised and wrong. The confident voice seemed friendly and respectful. He introduced himself as Richard, just a bloke from Canberra seeking advice for his son Toby who was at school and playing football in England. Shortly after his introduction, he asked me for my bank account details as he wanted to transfer money to me for my time. He told me he knew who I was, he had read my book, *Riding Shotgun*, and he said he was not looking to screw me over for free advice. I told him I didn't want any money from him, I was just happy to help him and his boy at a point in my life where I had realised that giving is the greatest gift.

But he wouldn't let up, so I said, "How about you buy a book for your son and we have a deal?"

He replied, "I'll buy a book for my son and 20 for my business executives."

"We've got a deal," I said. Unknown to me then, this small deal, this moment in time, would change my life in the coming months in a big way, more than I could ever have imagined. It delivered me Richard Peil, a friend, a brother, a lifeline!

In the coming weeks we began to chat a lot, not only about football but also life in general, with one common theme: Leeds United. The Leeds team poster from a *Shoot* magazine adorned my bedroom wall as a child, inspiring my dreams of one day playing at Elland Road, a dream that eventually came true.

Richard was born on a council estate in Leeds, the son of a 'Ten Pound Pom'. His dream of playing for Leeds never eventuated. His football career took him as far as Luton Town reserves when they were one of England's top three clubs, along with years of rough-and-tough football in the working-class city of Wollongong, its steel yards a constant reminder of a place not for the faint-hearted. Rich was a tough defensive midfielder who kicked more bodies than balls, took no prisoners and became one of the youngest footballers to play for an Australian National Soccer League club, the Wollongong Wolves. His football dream would fall short, but as all winners do, he found a passion and love for the fitness industry, creating his very own fitness empire by bringing the American 'Anytime Fitness' franchise down under.

We would talk for hours on end about football and fitness, sharing similar thoughts and a multitude of processes and methods around developing world-class football athletes. Around this time, the governing body of football in Canberra was advertising for a Football Director and Technical Director, so Rich kindly offered to create a CV for me to apply for the roles. In his words, "There would be no better man for the job." He truly believed it was criminal that I was not working in football, so he took it upon himself to help me.

I knew my CV was better than all the Canberra football coaches and administrators put together. Unfortunately, I also knew that Canberra in the last 20 or so years had become arguably the most toxic football community on the planet. With jealousy, self-interest and human insecurities rampant, the decision-makers at all levels never wanted anybody with any remote knowledge of football destroying their little castles or exposing their incompetence. Clubs against clubs, clubs and the governing body in never-ending battles, all seemingly wanting nothing more than demise for each other.

Of course, there are always a few good operators who try to help you but invariably they end up a silent minority protecting their own careers. It was a far cry from the wonderful Canberra football community I had grown up in. So, I was one hundred percent sure I would not get either of the roles on offer, I was simply too hot to handle for them both in a football sense and politically. I was right: another rejection, and although I knew it was coming, it still hurt more than you can ever imagine. You somehow create a false expectation in your mind in those situations, hoping and praying that you might be delivered the lifeline of an opportunity, but it never arrives. Smiling assassins are everywhere, many of them football nobodies; they are as cold as ice, like the Canberra winters they live in!

Conversations between Rich and I continued, and eventually we went down the path of creating our own A-League club in Canberra. A club that would possibly align in member partnerships with the Canberra Raiders and the ACT Brumbies. I put Rich in touch with Australian Professional Leagues' CEO, Danny Townsend, and discussions for the purchase of an A-League licence began, despite Canberra being a few years away from the possibility of joining the competition at the time. It was probably a bit early for the Canberra bid to progress, but both Rich and I had got to the stage where we wanted to purchase or buy into a football club. Well, he would anyway, because I was broke from years of cocaine abuse and all the bad financial choices that came with that.

I had self-sabotaged my career, with rumours and innuendo about anything and everything getting bigger by the day. I was unemployable in most cases, bringing in what money I could with occasional personal training, scouting work and labouring for tradesmen friends who would pay me more out of pity than anything else. I had no skills in their field but I gave them a world of hard work for a much needed dollar.

They were tough times, and like the Bon Jovi song, my wife, Jaynie, and I were 'living on a prayer'. I was down on my luck and she, like Gina, worked the diner all day; she always brought home her pay for love and kept us from drowning. My last decent pay day had come a few years earlier from Celtic FC as part of a Tom Rogic agency fee, but that too had gone quickly, helping to make our mortgage repayments. It would be the last agency fee I received from Tom after years of representing him from an unknown and unwanted teenager in Canberra to legend status at Celtic FC. We went our separate ways, and he signed for one of England's top agents who promised him the world and delivered him one season at West Bromwich Albion!

And then, as fate would have it, another phone call came out of the blue from an old opponent, author and now football commentator, Andy Harper. It would change our direction. His advice was to leave the Canberra bid for now and try to cut a deal with Mike Charlesworth, the UK-based owner of the Central Coast Mariners, something nobody else on the planet had been capable of achieving. A few Zoom meetings later and Rich had become chairman of the club, something many said was impossible: it's a word that both Rich and I are not synonymous with.

Shortly after, I travelled up to the Central Coast where Rich addressed the players and introduced me as part of his team. No role was discussed, I was just to be part of his crew, but he knew I carried a special magic with me, a glue that could unite and empower players and staff alike. Rich asked me to say a few words to the playing group, which I did, then handed them all a copy of my autobiography, *Riding Shotgun*. I told them to read it, study it, learn from it and be empowered by it.

It was on this day that I would first meet Nick 'Monty' Montgomery, who carried the same nickname as Field Marshal Bernard Montgomery, one of the most prominent and successful British commanders of the Second World War—only this Monty was a modern-day commander in charge of a football club. After spending the morning in his presence, I knew that I had to become one of his lieutenants in whatever capacity was required of me.

I've always studied the history of football so I knew about Monty's fantastic career and his legendary status at Sheffield United, but more impressive on this day was the content of his character. He's a good man with special managerial skills. A born leader, I immediately likened him to the great managers of the game I had met, played for or played against, like British legends Brian Clough and Alex Ferguson, the Real Madrid Spaniards, 'Pachin', Vicente del Bosque and Julen Lopetegui, and Australia's very own

Ange Postecoglou. He is of their ilk and at the time I met him, he was in the process of securing finals football in his first year as the Mariners' A-League Head Coach after earlier in the season leading them to the 2021–22 Australia Cup Final, narrowly losing to Melbourne Victory.

My role, whatever it was to be, would officially begin in the 2022–23 season. However, from the time I met him, Monty allowed me access to all areas, embracing me like I was part of his family. Honesty, loyalty and trust were three key traits that delivered us an immediate mutual respect, on top of having shared many similar football experiences in England.

I have always seen football as war, a consequence of growing up in a Spanish household where technical and physical attributes were valued extremely highly but going to war was not negotiable. My grandfather and father were military men, and Monty's father and grandfather were also military men, so going to war by his side would not only be a pleasure, but also an honour.

So, the son of Spanish immigrants was on the move again. A lifetime of global travelling was part of my family history, in my blood and part of my destiny. This time it would coincide with my re-entry to professional football in a place called the Central Coast in New South Wales. It's a paradise known for its beautiful beaches, palm trees, pretty girls and a football team who over the past decade had excelled in mediocrity, their trophy cabinet full of wooden spoons.

CHAPTER 2

DEAD AND GONE

AMERICAN RAPPER T.I. WROTE, "NO MORE STRESS, NOW I'M straight, time to think before I make mistakes just for my family's sake, that part of me left yesterday, the heart of me is strong today, no regrets I'm blessed to say, the old me dead and gone away." He was spot on.

So off we went to the Central Coast of New South Wales, about an hour's drive north of Sydney. A place once described to me by a few former Socceroo and Mariners' stars to be a place of beauty where nothing much happens but it's a really hard place to leave. Joining the Mariners was a real blessing for my wife, Jaynie. Despite being one of the best hospitality and event managers on the planet, her work was taking its toll physically and mentally. It's an industry where beautiful days were becoming far less the norm, and her beautiful spirit was ruined on many occasions by rude, horrible customers, and at times by bosses.

I'm not sure how to best describe the Central Coast. It's a multitude of small towns, places and villages, all thrown together alongside stunning beaches, lakes, canals, rivers and inlets, with a road system bearing more potholes and craters than you would find on the moon. I quickly found my way around, somehow joining all the dots of this geographical maze with ease.

Our first two places of residence were Copacabana and Terrigal, both boasting picturesque beaches. They are portraits of a beautiful land that people around the world would dream of visiting, and maybe one day living there. Yes, places of beauty and paradise, but also places built on hills and cliffs, more suited to a mountain goat than a human being, especially one with a lifelong dodgy knee like mine.

I longed for flatter and more level ground, and it came in the form of our third home in Chittaway Bay, but not before I had established a few great friendships with the locals in Terrigal. One in particular was a friend from many years ago, Lawrie McKinna, the former Head Coach and Football Director of the Mariners, and for a period of time, the Lord Mayor of Gosford. Lawrie actually gave me my first boot sponsorship while he was in charge at Asics Australia.

I didn't let him down either, winning the National Soccer League Grand

Final, and later playing in a packed Wembley Stadium for a place in the EPL (English Premier League) wearing the same Asics boots he had put in my Woollahra Council work ute years earlier. A diehard Glasgow Rangers fan and one of the world's greatest social butterflies, he led a group of swimmers every morning at Terrigal Beach. The self-titled team 'Scozzie' would swim in the rain, hail or shine. They are all beautiful people with their own wonderful stories.

I quickly gravitated towards two men who are both now great friends, Joel Cangy and Joe Coyte. Joel at times shared similar experiences to mine, and before I knew it, we were besties, attending events at the Glen Rehabilitation Centre and NRL (National Rugby League) Grand Finals, courtesy of his friend and business colleague, the legendary rocker Jimmy Barnes.

Joe Coyte is a beautiful man who gives his life to serving and helping others on a daily basis. He was the main man at the Glen, a place where I not only found peace, but our whole squad did too on regular visits. A big part of Monty's management is to help the community, others that are less fortunate, others who are doing it tough, and in the Glen's case, those with addictions.

We would go and spend time there as a team, listening to their stories and sharing our stories around the fireplace on Aboriginal land surrounded by Aboriginal artefacts, paintings and spirits. It's a place that leaves us empowered and humbled, traits that are the very essence of our club. For our semi-final versus Adelaide City, the Glen boys did a ceremonial dance and welcome to country ceremony that not only inspired our players, but also our fans. We felt their energy on their land, and we would not be defeated on our pitch.

Another beautiful person amongst this crazy lot was the Mariners' number one season ticket holder, *MasterChef Australia* winner Julie Goodwin. Julie, along with Lawrie, Joe and Joel, would hound me every day, wanting me to swim out to the buoy and back, but try as they may, I never succumbed. My answer to them was always, "I've come here to win the A-League, not be eaten by a shark!"

After enjoying the spoils of Terrigal for the first few months, we were off to our new house in Chittaway Bay. Not only was it a perfect location for work, being five minutes from the club's Centre of Excellence (COE), but it also came with a beautiful pool lined by even more beautiful palm trees right outside our bedroom. How cool was that? There were palm trees and ocean blue water at our stadium and the same at home; it was paradise every day.

With these surroundings, I could have been forgiven for thinking I had been reunited with David Beckham at his very own Inter Miami! It was a large house, so in addition to both Jaynie's and my duties at the club (Jaynie was now working in the Mariners' office), we created a boarding house, or 'digs' as they call them in the UK. Both Monty and I had at some stage spent time in digs, he at Sheffield United and me at Ipswich Town, so we thought this would be a wonderful asset for the club, a perfect spot for housing young interstate players. So, almost overnight, we became de facto parents to four young footballers who played in our Academy teams.

The Glen Rehab centre lay in between the COE and our house, the perfect location for me. I would visit regularly on the way home from training for a little something in the gym, or just to say hello to the lads. It made me feel good knowing that they might somehow be inspired by my presence, by my story and start seeing the sunshine again. I had been where they were, probably in far darker places than many of them, so if I could somehow be their beacon of light, of hope, then I told myself I must show my face as much as possible.

This road then led to helping out the Salvation Army and working with the NSW Police Force and PCYC (Police Citizens Youth Club) on a 'fit for life' campaign to help young kids from broken homes dealing with addictions and heading in the wrong direction. One Salvation Army mission took Jaynie and me to the Dooralong Transformation Centre where I spoke to a full chapel of men struggling with addictions just before Christmas. Initially they were sceptical; all they could see was some bloke in a Mariners' tracksuit preaching to them about life, until I began trumping their addictions with my own. It was very spiritual, especially when I told them about my crack cocaine days, giving them specifics of how I would cook the crack then smoke it in homemade pipes made from mini-bar whisky bottles.

At that point, I had their full attention. I had their souls, and more importantly, their trust. I was just like them, but I had changed my life. I was the living proof they could change too. Before I left, I gave them all a copy of my book, *Riding Shotgun*, and told them to read it. It personifies resilience, something they would all need in bundles to save their own lives. On the way out, I turned to Jaynie and said, "Did you see their faces light up? Did you see how much love they gave us? Did you see the hope in their eyes?" It was one of the best things I have ever done in my life and one of the best days of my life, giving me more joy than any football match I ever played in.

PCYC visits were mostly to gyms. I would take injured players with me, and we would do fitness and boxing with the young kids, hoping that they would see sports and fitness as a different road than the one they were on (that for many was one headed straight to jail, and in some cases, death).

On one occasion the police brought a whole busload of young girls to our A-League training session and Monty allowed them to do the team warm-up with the players. Senior police officers that day would tell me that they had never seen anything like it before. Firstly, the inclusion, and secondly, the positive impact it had on those young girls.

On the back of this, I was honoured to be invited as a special guest of the Wyong Police Station for a bike presentation to a young Aboriginal lad doing great work in the community as a Special Constable. How my life had changed. In the past 15 years I had run from police, been locked up by police, at times helped and been screwed over by police. Now I was rolling through Wyong Police Station at peace with the world, the pin-up boy of the force!

Jaynie was now working as a PA to both the CEO, Shaun Mielekamp, and Chairman, Richard Peil, in a business that she loved. The football staff and players made her one of their team immediately. They loved her and a lot of unseen work she did for them would play a big part in the club's wonderful season. Besides hosting the Chairman's Lounge on match days, she helped the foreign legion find suitable housing and schools, and even with the purchasing of cars. On the eve of our home semi-final against Adelaide United, together with Sporting Director Matt Simon, we even found ourselves doing a late-night, end-of-lease furniture removal and clean-up!

Anything and everything at any time was part of every employee's job description. On one occasion, we headed to Newcastle to buy a second-hand car for one of the foreigners. Not only were we going into enemy territory, but we ended up in the dodgiest car dealership I've ever seen. Walking into the place, the dealer led us to the Peugeot that we were supposed to buy. It was a complete shitbox that smelt like an oily rag and drove no better. It had no logbook and was missing many parts (an important one being the gear stick lever—a screwdriver doing the job instead). It was definitely not the same car that had been advertised online!

Jaynie had grown up around cars, her dad, David, being the 1974 Australian speedway champion, so there was no way she was falling for this one. She said, "If you give this bloke even one cent, we are finished." So, any money I had in my pocket stayed there. We returned home empty-handed, but a few weeks later the same car somehow ended up in the COE car park, now being used by one of our imports. The Mariners' madness was never-ending, baffling even my mad mind at times.

A short time later, in enemy territory once again for the Newcastle 500 V8 Supercar series, we would find ourselves (courtesy of our good friend Gary Reid) standing on the track next to superstar racing car drivers

Shane Van Gisbergen and Cam Waters pre-race for the national anthem. The Australian Air Force fighter jets flying overhead almost blew the eardrums out of our heads but insanely, we wanted them to do it one more time. It was a truly magical moment. The extremes of our car dealings had no limits and no bounds—from shitboxes to million-dollar racing machines—but they reflected the club itself. We had no limits and no bounds either, we turned everything into gold.

For me, the most important thing was that my wife was happy. To all the lads, and their wives or partners, she was like a big sister or mother, and whatever needed to be done, she did with a "Hello, darling" and a big smile on her face. So, as they say, happy wife, happy life.

More cars came and it now seemed like we were starting a Mariners' used car dealership. In addition, a friend of mine and former Young Socceroo, Zoran Ilic (Managing Director of ISS Shipping), had kindly donated shipping containers that we would eventually use to build our gyms, so at one point our training complex was looking more like Port Botany's international shipping docks than a football training complex. Bargain buys, donations and doing any job that needed to be done was the reality of how the lowest-budget club rolled.

On the football side, it was a fascinating new adventure. I immediately got on great with Monty's number two, Sergio 'Serg' Raimundo, the well-travelled Portuguese coaching wizard, who is a beautiful man too. I had seen Carlos Queiroz work at Real Madrid and Serg was at that level and more. He was always looking for the edge, pushing boundaries, planning sessions, cutting clips long into the early hours of the morning and seeking perfection in destroying opposition teams. A former Marine, he knew five languages, loved unarmed combat and was the perfect foil and partner for Monty. He had previously worked at Benfica, arguably one of the world's greatest producers of football talent. That in itself told a story. He wasn't a manager; he was a proper coach. A tactician well versed in the art of war; a master chess player of the highest order.

As is the norm with football, there would be comings and goings, both staff and players. We would add Brice Johnson as Head of Strength and Conditioning, along with Miguel Miranda, a Goalkeeping Coach who we likened to a Portuguese Mr. Bean. He's a very clever 'bean' though, and a world-class developer of keepers. Brice had previously been at the Mariners and was now returning after a spell with our archrivals, the Jets, who proved to be dumber than dumb when releasing such a world-class fitness guru and also one of the greatest blokes you could ever meet.

Darren Dobson (aka Dobbo), the Team Manager, Kit Man, the GOAT, was an immovable and irreplaceable force. Stamati Glaros, Video Analyst and Scouting, youngster Liam Chauncy, Analyst and Drone Pilot, Coach Lucas Vilela ('mini Serg'), Assistant Strength and Conditioning Coach Cade Mapu, and physiotherapists John Donelly and Nick Van Reede made up the team.

The one constant in all these men was that apart and away from football they are good men, good souls. People, coaches and clubs always talk about setting standards, setting a bar and creating a culture, but these things can only ever be attained with good people. One rotten egg, one bit of cancer within the staff or within the playing group and it's game over; you won't win shit!

So where would I fit in? Richard had always seen me as the Head of Athletic Development; after all, that was my specialty, my love. Since my Little Athletics days, and then as part of the Australian Institute of Sport (AIS) Football Program, I was always passionate about the gym/strength side of football. For the 2012 London Olympic Games, I delivered both the track work and strength programs for the Australian boxing team, so I would take much of that knowledge and mindset into the Mariners' setup. I would sit in between Monty and Brice creating what we called 'Central Coast Machines'.

With Brice, I would deliver gym sessions either group-based or individually. But more importantly, I would do whatever the players did, leading the way by example. Words are cheap, so if the boys could see me at my age doing the hard yards, then it would hopefully be a source of inspiration for them and leave them with no excuses.

Bottom line, to play for us you would need to be or become a world-class athlete, and as harsh as it seems, my job was to eradicate or eliminate the mentally and physically weak; they would not be for us. Like NFL special teams but on an individual basis, I would work one-on-one with the players, mentoring them, helping them in whatever way was necessary.

Monty and Serg had the football sessions covered, they didn't need my help in that department, but they were always open to any football knowledge that I sometimes brought to the table. For me, watching them at work after disappearing from planet Earth for over a decade was like going to university again. During my AIS playing days, I began a Sports Administration degree at the University of Canberra, but I never completed it after I signed on as a professional footballer in Spain. But I was now looking at session plans, watching match previews and reviews of a quality I had never seen before, not even at Real Madrid. I knew time had moved on, but these guys were pushing the boundaries of football planning. It was for footballers what aeronautical engineering was to astronauts. So, I would sit amongst the players as I had done years before and listen, sponge and educate myself further. Wise men will tell you if you're the smartest guy in the room you're in trouble, so I was loving being around men far smarter than myself.

The greatest thing about working alongside Monty and Serg was that they just let me be me. Jason Cummings would tell you that I was the glue that brought everything together. It's a very humbling comment but I suppose that's what I did. I can't tell you the secret formula or what methods I put in place, they just came naturally. I just did me, did weights with the players, did ice baths with them, did sauna recovery with them, did boxing with them, and told them stories every day. My life stories, everything good and bad that I had been through, emptying my soul so as to help them become better professionals, and better men capable of one day grasping their own dreams as I once had.

With the coaches, I was everybody's lieutenant. They all knew my football CV and they all highly respected me. For that, I gave them my full respect, loyalty, trust and everything a man could give. They all knew I had their backs and when it was time to go to war or anything else, I was more than happy to go first.

It was around this time that Monty would bestow the title 'Vibe Manager' upon me, something that would haunt Melbourne City's Scott Jamieson for life by the end of the Grand Final. At first, we had a laugh about it, but a week later Jaynie Googled 'vibe manager' and we quickly realised that Microsoft, Google and the Hard Rock Café chain all have one. It was a thing, and I was now the first one in world football. A few months later, the Socceroos would appoint Martin Boyle as their Vibe Manager, but like being the first Australian to play in Spain, and the first to captain an English football club, I now had another first that I'm very proud of—and as we all know, if you're not first, you're last!

We had lost players, very important ones in the off-season, so how would we replace them? Would we be more or less competitive? Only time would tell; the only thing I knew for sure was that Monty and Sergio were relentless in striving for success and I was alive and kicking, not dead and gone as many fools believed.

CHAPTER 3

RETURN TO SENDER

PRE-SEASON BEGAN AND WE IMMEDIATELY TOOK THE TEAM to Canberra—my birthplace and my home for the past decade. We stayed at the Australian Institute of Sport's halls of residence and used the facilities that for the past 40 years have produced some of the greatest sportsmen and sportswomen this country has ever seen. We played two matches in two weeks. We defeated reigning ACT NPL champions Monaro Panthers 5–0, then the following week we beat a Capital Football NPL All Stars team 4–1. They were decent results when, to be honest, we were operating at 30 or 40% of where we would need to be for the start of the season.

For the Canberra teams, it was an opportunity to pit themselves against an A-League team, and for us, it was the beginning of creating a team bond and system of play that all the players would buy into and become familiar with. In addition to the slog of pre-season fitness training, which itself was very tough, the cold Canberra winter provided an uncomfortable dynamic that most of the boys hated, but which they had no other choice than to embrace.

On a daily basis they would ask me how I had lived here for two years during my AIS days. I reminded them that I was born in Canberra, the first 18 years of my life were spent in the city, and I had grown to make the cold my friend. In the summer it would be oppressively hot and there was little in between, so from a young age I created a mindset that if it was cold I wanted it colder, if it was hot I wanted it hotter, knowing that my opponents, especially the weaker ones, would give me their souls.

It was here that for the first time I would meet a gentleman called Ezio Mormile. He is the most beautiful, wonderful human you could ever meet, and he was our Mindset Coach. Ezio would always wear the same shirt, a blue-and-yellow-chequered number he had bought in Naples, Italy, a few years back, not long after he had first met Monty. He bought it in honour of Monty's Scottish heritage but it was actually made in Portugal, linking it in some divine way to our other coaches, Serg and Miguel. His wife thought it was awful, so based on that opinion, Ezio decided to buy it and wear it every time he was in our presence. It was a part of him that became a source of comfort, security and power for every single one of us.

THE VIBE MANAGER

The biggest honour and tribute I can bestow upon him is that on Mad Monday after we had won the Grand Final, all the lads wore a shirt exactly like the one Ezio would always wear, topped off with a bald cap to look as close as possible to the man himself. The icing on the cake was that each player's nickname given to them by Ezio had been pressed onto the back of their shirts. Jason Cummings would impersonate him so perfectly on many occasions that you couldn't tell the difference in both mannerisms and voice. They say impersonation or imitation is the greatest form of flattery, and in Ezio's case, it went way above. We all love and adore him. "Family" as he would say!

Ezio grabbed me early on and we discussed how we could help the boys, both as a group and as individuals. Coffee after coffee after coffee, one thousand coffees later, by the end of the season we knew exactly the animals that we had and what made them tick. It was mental empowerment, the likes of which I had never seen or encountered before, except in my own mind at times.

The great managers can bring staff and players together to buy into the same vision, agree on similar processes and put them into practice, even if they seem unconventional or uncomfortable. This ability was one of Monty's many strengths and one evening after consulting with him, Ezio and I took a carefully selected group of boys to the outdoor pool at my old apartment. We only went there because the recovery centre at the AIS was booked out and there was no way the boys were missing their session. Trust me, if my apartment pool had not been available, I planned to put them into Lake Burley Griffin, whose waters in the middle of winter are as cold as the North Atlantic Sea.

When we arrived, the water temperature must have been around zero and the boys were not happy, most of them not sure what to think of this lunatic Andy Bernal. To them, it seemed like madness and something that they would not be capable of doing. It was beyond their understanding of recovery methods, but for Ezio and myself, it was more than recovery. It was about who goes in first, 'one in, all in', family and togetherness. Words that Ezio would use as a masterstroke weeks out from the Grand Final, linking them to our mobile phones in a way none of us could have ever imagined.

Nobody was going in, so I led the way and jumped in first, followed by Ezio. At that point, the lads had no choice. If we could do it, they could do it too. To be honest, it was so cold that Jason started singing, a way of eliminating the pain of the freezing cold water. They say your body can only survive in arctic waters for a few minutes and they're right, that's all we managed, but it was done as a group singing 'Stand By Me'. It was at this moment that

THE VIBE MANAGER

I knew the power of Ezio and the mental fortitude of the players, especially the leaders, Jason Cummings and Matt Simon.

This would be Matt's final hurrah as a player, unfortunately; a neck injury would force him into early retirement. In another masterstroke, Monty would transition him into the role of Sporting Director, and he became a very good one at that. It showed the lads and all of us that Matt, even in his moment of mental torture, contemplating a life without playing football anymore and not knowing at this point where his life was headed, would still get into the freezing water. The message was the Mariners were family, we stood for a greater cause. It was about the club, the community and your teammates. The individual mattered, but only as part of a greater unit.

It was during this camp that we began formulating special projects where I would take charge. Two priority projects were Jason Cummings and Matheus Moresche, who would between them score four goals in the Grand Final. Moresche was a long-term project, he had many months of ACL rehabilitation ahead of him, so Jason was priority number one. He had returned from his off-season Bali rampage overweight and unfit, to say the least, but after Monty and I spoke to him with both empathy and understanding, he embraced anything and everything extra that I gave him. In these initial weeks, we began to work with and understand each other. It was a coming together of two crazy minds that just worked.

We would chat for hours on subjects that were far from football, and his intelligence had no boundaries. If I brought up ancient Rome, he would name the Emperors. If I brought up presidents of the United States, he would name them in order. If I brought up Frank Sinatra, he would immediately sing 'I Did It My Way' and not miss a word! A tattoo of his dog Carlos, the Joker on his hand and one of superstar Olivia Newton-John from his favourite movie *Grease* adorned his body and were examples of how weird and wonderful his mind is.

I once told him he reminded me of a fantastic Celtic striker who moved to Arsenal and before I had a chance to name him, he replied with "Champagne Charlie Nicholas"! Jason wasn't even born when Charlie was playing at Highbury (Arsenal's old stadium) and frequenting London's nightclubs but somehow, he knew of him. He did history very well. He had a genial brain; hanging out with him was like playing *The Chase* and he was the Chaser!

He was also a warrior and very strong-willed, so I could not and did not break him, as much as I tried. The gym wasn't his place of choice but he had the ability to do any exercise with the technical precision and as much loading as the best in our squad, it was just a matter of pushing the right buttons. In the wrong hands he would give nothing, but in the right hands he would superset every machine in the gym.

On a football level, he reminded me of the legendary Real Madrid and Spanish international striker Raul, who could play 9 or as a false 9 equally well. On top of all the football training and pre-season running, we boxed ourselves silly to a point where Jason would call out Jake Paul for a boxing bout, and he was deadly serious. I knew if Jake put up a few million dollars, we were on our way to Vegas! The kilos began to come down, his overall fitness went up and now he was in line for a Socceroos World Cup squad selection. Graham Arnold picked him, and then he was off to Qatar, achieving what many footballers dream of, but only a few achieve.

In the middle of all the facilities was a statue of two footballers based on a photo of Socceroos' legend Frank Farina (the first Australian to play in Italy) and myself (the first Australian to play in Spain) tackling him when we were both at the AIS. The boys were pretty impressed with that; they were getting to know me a little more day by day, and I loved that they respected my achievements, hoping it would serve to educate and inspire them.

The cold days and nights began to get a little easier for the boys. Adaptation is a must for any footballer wanting to go far in this game. After playing the All Stars' match, a party at Chairman Richard's house in Red Hill would again be a test. Yes, we had a party, but not before making the boys jump into the freezing pool that must have been below zero around 10 p.m. that night!

With Canberra done and dusted, we left the city I grew up in as I had done many years before. In the distance, the white-capped peaks of the snowy mountains had me hungry for new peaks to conquer. One in particular: to become the A-League champions.

CHAPTER 4

THE CUP

THE AUSTRALIA CUP DRAW CAME EARLY FOR US AND revealed we would play Sydney FC in the Round of 32. It was a strange feeling on a football level as we entered this game still in pre-season mode and far from the levels required from our players during the regular season. In England, the FA Cup matches that I played in were always aligned with the normal season, so this was new to me. It is what it is though, and with the NPL (National Premier league) and A-League playing in two different seasons, one in winter and one in summer, it will always create unbalanced and ill-timed match-ups, but it's the nature of Australian football, I suppose.

For me, it would be my first official game back involved in professional football. It came with the added excitement of my sister Raquel and nephew Lucas visiting from New York. After all I had been through in my life, I was proud of where I was now, and they were too. I couldn't wait to share this day with them. All the heartache I had put them through was eradicated in one moment as the Mariners' bus arrived at Leichhardt Oval, my old stomping ground, and I gave them their tickets for the match. It felt great being part of this show; I hadn't had this feeling since my playing days at Reading FC and boy, how I had missed it!

A year earlier, the team had made it to the Cup Final, losing to Melbourne Victory with a few controversial decisions that would add fuel to our fire for all this season's upcoming competitions. Both teams had players that had at some point played for the other side, so it added a little further spark to the match too. We played quite well that day, despite not having the first 11 we desired and that we would eventually have. We were two men down at one point via a send-off and an injury, but our nine men took them all the way to penalties.

At this point, the match became a lottery, with Sydney FC's keeper and former Mariner and World-Cup-bound Socceroo Andrew Redmayne winning the game for them with important saves, a product of ridiculous and embarrassing movement on the line that is now outlawed by FIFA, the game's global governing body. They were the same antics that saw Australia through to the World Cup in their final qualification match against Peru, so whatever he was doing was working.

If it got the Socceroos to the World Cup then I would run with it; I had no choice, you have to support the lads and your nation. Personally, I didn't like it; for my money it was not in the spirit of the game but my opinion didn't matter, and bottom line, all is fair in love and war! The media loved it though, they dubbed him the 'grey Wiggle' and for a while that Wiggle shit received more television exposure than football itself.

But in that defeat, we found empowerment. We deserved more against one of the nation's best football clubs, and it would spur us on to greater days. For me it was a beautiful night. I had found an ally in FIFA, the very same governing body whose antiquated rules many years ago had robbed me of a long Spanish career and resulted in my United Kingdom deportation.

I had now returned to football as part of a wonderful coaching team at one of the most iconic and historical grounds in Australia, where I had played many games in the old National Soccer League. Jason gave my nephew Lucas his signed shirt and it now hangs in New York, awaiting a visit from the Joker himself. The fairy-tale football return was incomplete through defeat but a grander fairy tale lay ahead, one that not even Walt Disney himself could have imagined.

After a nice evening in Darling Harbour, it was back to the coast to prepare for the season proper. Macarthur Bulls, led by my old mate Dwight

Yorke, went on to win the Cup, but to this day I believe that if we had got past Sydney that night, we would have won it ourselves; there's not a single doubt in my mind.

CHAPTER 5
WINDOWS AND CLOSETS

IN THE WEEK LEADING UP TO THE GRAND FINAL, MY FRIEND Vince Rugari would write a piece titled 'Misshapes, mistakes and misfits: How Toy Story explains the Central Coast Mariners' in the *Sydney Morning Herald*. He described how we had put together a team worthy of an A-League Grand Final on a shoestring budget by sifting through trash and finding treasure. He likened it to the Hollywood movie *Moneyball*, ingenuity in its truest sense, and the art of coaching at its finest.

He wrote, "The Mariners are a collection of misshapes, mistakes and misfits all of whom have been deemed defective or incomplete at some time of their careers, tossed aside as football junk – only for a coach in Nick Montgomery to see and understand their worth, rescue these offcuts, and create something not just new, but truly special."

Players come and go, coaches come and go; it's the nature of the business we call football. Sometimes it happens in pre-season, sometimes mid-season and sometimes at the end of the season, but in nearly every case, it's never personal, it's just business. Some players that you think are right end up being wrong and you must eradicate them quickly. They may not adapt to the environment or culture or perform to the standards required. Some players like Garang Kuol create global attention and are purchased by the giants of world football. The merry-go-round of incoming and outgoing footballers is an industry in itself. It's a constant part of the global game.

If you're looking for new talent and looking to get rid of players, then your global scouting network must be of the highest order. Modern-day methods of data interpretation and analytics are also important, along with multilingual staff capable of conversing in the many languages of the world. Contacts, connections built up over years and years in the business, will eventually lead to face-to-face dialogue and meetings, where ultimately the content of character is the key.

We had lost quite a few important players: Mark Birighitti, Lewis Miller, Noah Smith, Costa Rica international Marcos Ureña, former Socceroo Oliver Bozanic and current Socceroo Kye Rowles. In the mid-season break, we would also lose Garang to Newcastle United. These are all very good players and hard to replace. Replace them we did though, with astute and clever signings that would make us an even better side.

We brought in Danny Vukovic, Sammy Silvera, Marco Tulio, Brian Kaltak and Nectar Triantis, who would all play key roles and star for us throughout the season. Yet many external voices initially spoke of them as being over the hill, past their best, failed wonderkids and never-beens. The art of working with footballers like these is where the magic exists. It's an ability that some coaches have, and one that many will never have. It's a gift that can't be taught, it comes from the soul and is used to fix broken players and nurse others into the world-class performances they can deliver.

It's a double-edged sword though, this football business, and transfer periods bring up many varied human emotions. As soon as you fix or further develop players to perform at very high levels, they attain success and with that comes interest from other clubs. Sometimes this is done respectfully and sometimes not, as was the case with our superstar Brian Kaltak. So outstanding were his performances that representatives from one of our rival clubs spoke to him directly on the day we were playing them at home.

I've been in the deals that took Beckham to Real Madrid and Tim Cahill to Everton, moves that were procured and concluded respectfully by all parties, so you can't trick a trickster. Neither our club nor I will ever tolerate approaches being made to our players without our consent and without going through the proper channels and processes first. If another club comes to us in the right manner, then it's a business transaction. If not, it's a piss-take and they will be told that in no uncertain terms.

Somehow on the evening of that match, I found trouble again after approaching the offending club's Director of Football and CEO in the tunnel after the match. I had been longing for this moment all night and it finally came with a few heated words, but not much else. It was nothing too drastic, it looked way worse than it was as I was escorted away by our Chairman and a few NSW police officers on duty that night.

At least on this occasion I wasn't put in handcuffs as had been done to me years ago while playing for Sydney Olympic against Wollongong Wolves in the old National Soccer League. Of course, it got back to A-League headquarters, the hierarchy giving me a slap on the wrist and a stern warning, but I had made my point. We as a club will never be stepped on or bullied, either on the football pitch or off it. Not on my watch.

Our coaching unit had all the above qualities individually, but it was never enough alone, so we all constantly looked to help each other and better ourselves in all facets of the business. Matt Simon took to the Sporting Director role like a duck to water. He's a very intelligent man, a multi-skilled 'learn as you go' kind of guy that can one minute build an outdoor gym, and the next conclude an important international transfer. I have previously worked as an agent managing David Beckham, Tim Cahill and Tom Rogic, so he also had all my experience and knowledge available to him if needed.

Monty, Serg and Miguel brought their world of connections to Matt's table, and in Jordan Smith, the Mariners' legal eagle, he had one of the world's best lawyers to assist him with legalities. He was now in a role he loved, in his town, at the club he loved. He had fully transitioned from playing to one of the most important figures within the organisation, and he was good. So good that a few months later he would win the Chairman's Award, with everybody else at the club a distant second.

In some cases, you need to move players on. Players who just aren't performing, are rotten eggs or cancerous souls who can destroy a dressing room even before a ball is kicked. There are ways and methods for this; it's not easy, but we did it well and always respectfully. To the ones who left, we always wished them the best, and again, it was not personal, but they didn't fit in so they had to go.

We cleaned out our closet in the January window, bringing in James McGarry, Christian Theoharous and Dylan Wenzel-Halls. In this new trifecta we had three fine footballers, but they had come to us physically and mentally broken. I wondered if those who had broken them had done it on purpose. We will never know but it's something that happens in football; I know first-hand because it was something that was tried on me while I was playing for Reading FC.

Whatever the case, we would fix them, shower them with love and respect, and soon their once sad faces began to light up again. Dylan unfortunately got injured in his first ever training session with us and played only limited minutes in the final run, but his presence kept all the other strikers on their toes! Theoharous and McGarry would light up the League; they are exceptional talents worthy of many international caps for their respective countries down the track. All three became A-League champions with us, when months earlier they were on the football scrapheap. That's how we rolled. 'Family', remember.

CHAPTER 6

LET'S RIDE

 I WAS SUPER EXCITED FOR THE START OF THE SEASON. We had done plenty of hard work and I knew the football would take care of itself. For me, the many anecdotes and stories that always go side by side with the actual football are as important as the game itself, and they would come in many ways.

My first task was a special mission and nothing really to do with football itself. Monty asked me to chaperone Jason to Melbourne for the A-League season launch. It came with only one message and that was to get him back home safe and sound. That's easier said than done and it took me back to 2003 when my job was to chaperone David Beckham around the wonderful city of Madrid. In those days I would work together with David against thousands of global paparazzi, overzealous fans and the occasional threat of a possible kidnap attempt on his children. But this new mission was a whole different ball game and it focused on me safeguarding Jason from himself.

It was a great couple of days staying at the Crown Casino Hotel and filming at Ultra Football's headquarters. In the evenings, there were a few occasions where Jason would lose me (or at least, that's what he thought). This beautiful city comes with a heavy underground, a darker side. It's steeped in gangland wars and heavy hitters not to be messed with, so I made sure the places where he was headed would look after him and keep him from harm's way. I knew exactly where he was, knew when he left the hotel and when he got back. When he asked me how I knew, I told him Fidel Castro's former intelligence officers who were part of Beckham's security detail had taught me well. Season launch over and mission accomplished, we headed back to the coast.

As the opening game of the season approached, with it came the warmer weather and our morning ritual of backyard cricket. A bat, a ball and moveable stumps were all we needed, and the game served as a great mood enhancer before the whole squad commenced their pre-activation session. The usual suspects — Harry Steele, Yaren Sozer, Danny Vukovic, Jason Cummings and I — were the keenest.

As great a footballer as Jason is, he is equally as bad a cricketer, but he loves it and would provide running commentary as we played. He had a fascination with Shane Warne, but even more so with Freddie Flintoff, and every hit or catch he managed to make would come with a shout of "Freddie Flintoff". Who was to know that on Grand Final day, one of our finest cricket legends, the great Steve Waugh, would watch us play from the Chairman's box? We had played football against each other as kids; now linked by the Mariners, it seemed the cricket gods were doing their thing too!

Before things got too busy, I contacted Football Australia about finishing my Football Australia/AFC A Diploma. I had already done the first part while still in Canberra and simply wanted to complete part two. It would give me further education and it's always an added bonus to have around a football club. They came back to me with course dates, and of course, the dates clashed with the A-League Grand Final. So, I told them I wouldn't be there because we were going to play in that very same Grand Final! I'm not sure if they cared or didn't care, but they didn't try to work with me in obtaining my Diploma. Quite frankly, they probably thought I was nuts.

Surely they could have given me some form of credit or dispensation for being part of a Grand Final coaching staff, I thought to myself. No, and no way the Mariners would make it, they must have told themselves. They had previously fast-tracked others and were now fast-tracking other former Socceroos at the same time, so why not me? Why set a date that may have coaches in the A-League sphere not able to attend? Will this happen again next season? It was so ridiculous, but I was beyond getting annoyed, and I can't wait to catch up with Football Australia CEO James Johnson one day, so he can maybe answer my questions. I suppose for now I'll just keep winning things without that piece of paper!

Meanwhile, I somehow got conned into playing in the club's annual office staff versus football staff match. I hadn't played football for years and my left knee had been pretty much ready for a replacement 30 years ago! Although for many it was a fantastic and fun day, I went home miserable, in pain and depressed, having not been able to do what I once could. Monty was the top man, running around like he was back playing for Sheffield United, and the surprise package of the day was Miguel Miranda, our Goalkeeper Coach, who sat in at number six looking very much like the great Sergio Busquets.

Personally, I found it to be a nightmare. It was a horrible day and it haunted me for a few weeks until I was again somehow lured into another match. This time a 7 v 7 for a charity called 'Kicking Goals for Sick Kids', run and organised by a friend of mine and Mariners' club sponsor, George Shalal. It didn't take much to lure me in, because it was a wonderful cause that I would do anything for. I formed part of a top-flight team that included Nick Montgomery, Matt Simon, Luke Wilkshire, Nick Carle, Mile

THE VIBE MANAGER

Sterjovski, Patrick Zwaanswijk and Nicolai Muller. The only problem was we needed a goalkeeper, so you know who put his hand up! It wasn't my first rodeo, I'd previously played in goal for Sydney Olympic in the old NSL days and Reading FC in England, so I put the gloves on, made a few saves, and watched our boys put on a show from in between the posts. We had a blinder to be honest and we capped the night off with beer, kebabs and freshly made jam donuts, with any lingering depression from my last outing gone forever.

The season proper commenced with an F3 Derby against our bitter rivals, the Newcastle Jets. The rain gods were out in full force that day, and in a very short space of time our pitch was looking more like the bay across the road, leaving players and punters heading home in a world of disappointment with the match postponed.

Next up we travelled to Wellington in New Zealand, and for me it was a chance to catch up with my daughter Isabella and granddaughter Zoe. They flew from their home in Auckland and spent the weekend in the team hotel, watching us play our first game of the season in the wonderful stadium known as the 'Cake Tin'. All the players and coaching staff were friendly and welcoming to them, and it reinforced to me again how our own families are such an important part of our football team, our football family.

For me, it was a special moment. I was back in football and I'm pretty sure Isabella loved seeing me well and in my happy space again. The day before match day I spent with the girls playing on swings, eating vanilla ice creams and enjoying the beautiful Wellington Harbour. We gave away a late equaliser the next day which soured the afternoon a little, but nobody could take away the joy my heart felt playing with my granddaughter on the pitch after the final whistle had blown.

It was at this point in time that I began to recognise a greater picture beyond our football. It came in a simple but powerful word: 'family'. The season itself would bring wins and losses, creating much joy and much sadness at times, but we knew our football family was strong and could weather any storm, good or bad. For me, with our best players available, we were unbeatable. More important though were the off-field events and happenings that continued one after the other and created a strong, loving, unbreakable camaraderie that would lead to the ultimate goal and success.

Monty's father Tony came out a few months later and the team embraced him in the very same manner. One of his first trips away was to the country town of Mudgee. He travelled on the team bus as a member of our team; that's how we rolled. The night before the match, Tony and I found an Irish pub and exchanged many war stories. 'The gaffer's' dad needed to be looked after, so that's what I did as the Vibe Manager. Beer, whisky and a few cigarettes were all he needed; he's a simple but good man.

That match was a turning point in the season. We were struggling a bit with injuries and suspensions and were forced into playing a few of the scholars and young Academy boys. They all did great, and we spanked Macarthur Bulls 4–1. The result capped off a great weekend that in between football had Tony and I driving around the Mudgee countryside exploring vineyards, sheep and cattle stations.

About a month later, we travelled into country Victoria to the old mining town of Ballarat, only this time the match was on the same day that Tony was travelling back to England. Monty asked me if I could miss the match and get his father to the airport safely and securely. Tony had become my good friend in a short space of time, and it was my pleasure, but more than that it once again reinforced what a family we were. Whatever it took to make every single member of the team happy and comfortable, that's what we did. It was vibe management at its finest, and again we would do well in the bush, this time defeating reigning champions Western United.

Easter came and with it came Jaynie's mother, Eileen, for a little visit. This family thing again, it was always by our side. Eileen's sister Pat was the Mother Provincial of the Sisters of the Sacred Heart in Australia for many years. That means the top nun in the country! They are a very religious family, so with this in mind, Jaynie and I decided to take Eileen for Easter Mass at St Cecilia's Catholic Church in Wyong.

We arrived early, around 7 a.m., and parked the Mariners' A-League Isuzu Ute right out the front. By the end of the mass, the priest and all the congregation were Mariners' fans and waving us goodbye with prayers from the big man above. I thought it was a good omen; after all, Argentina had won the World Cup and we all know where the Pope is from!

Around semi-final time, my birthday approached. For me, it was always a dark day, many of them spent alone in Spain and England many years ago. Blocking them out as just another day helped erase and nullify the pain I was going through. Jaynie was in Canberra on some personal business and again I would be alone, although I had begun to deal with it a lot better these days.

As much as I tried to hide my birthday, Monty found out and called me after a mid-week training session, telling me he was taking me out to dinner. I wanted to say no, wanted to make an excuse, but it's something I couldn't do to him so reluctantly I agreed. What I didn't know was that he had also invited Serg and Abbas Saad, my old Sydney Olympic teammate when we won the Grand Final back in 1990. Abbas had joined the club a few months earlier to head up our wonderful Academy teams.

Now there were four of us, and Monty's pizza with just me was beginning to look like the very thing I was dreading—a party. But the clever fox wasn't finished yet and as we prepared to order, in came Jason and Steeley (Harry Steele), two of the boys that I am closest to and love dearly. Where previously I would have hated this scenario, strangely, a peace, joy and happiness came over me like never before. I was living a birthday that was very special, without any dark thoughts.

Once again it personified the man Monty is and the camaraderie and family that is part of the club's fabric. The evening ended in spectacular fashion with the owner telling Jason he would give him $5,000 if he scored a hat-trick in the Grand Final, and true to his word, weeks later he paid up!

With our best team on the pitch, we were invincible. The referees tried their best to eliminate us, or more to the point, to eliminate our wonderful centre-half Brian Kaltak. It got to the point where if he dared to look at an opponent, he ran the risk of a yellow or red card. His three send-offs were not send-off offences. They hurt us; he was our rock and without him we were a much inferior team. So, when he returned, he adapted — that's what good players do — and Monty's Player of the Year went on to create a story of never giving up that would inspire and give hope to millions of young children all over the Pacific Islands. As Brian adapted, so did the referees, and it seemed that as the season progressed, we began getting a fairer rub of the green.

Games came and went. We created our own mini leagues and tables within the competition. They were smaller goals and achievements that in the weeks to come would tell a bigger and greater story. A story of a team, the youngest in the League, who truly believed winning the Championship was possible, contrary to what most media outlets, pundits and so-called experts had predicted.

CHAPTER 7

BRICK WALLS AND COCONUTS

56 **IT WAS TIME FOR THE QATAR WORLD CUP IN 2022. THREE** of our players were selected: Jason Cummings, Garang Kuol and Danny Vukovic. All three would be part of a Socceroos squad that did its nation proud, and Garang would become the youngest player since the great Brazilian legend Pelé to appear in the knockout stages of the World Cup. It was incredible for both him and our club. We were also the only team in the history of the A-League to have three players from the one club in the Socceroos' World Cup squad, even though we are the smallest club with the youngest team. That was simply a world-class achievement.

The late addition of Melbourne City's Marco Tilio meant that the League giants would equal us, but reality would tell you that the only giant in this match-up was our achievement. For young Garang, his selection would also secure him a life-changing move to EPL side Newcastle United, a move that many believed would be hugely detrimental to our chances moving forward. He was outstanding and impressive off the bench for us before his move. A key weapon, he would be a big loss, but we would adapt; it's what you must do to survive in this game.

With the A-League shut down during the World Cup, we decided to take the boys to Vanuatu, the island paradise and birthplace of our star defender, Brian Kaltak, aka 'The Brick Wall of Gosford'. It was one trip that both Matt Simon and I had to unfortunately miss out on. With our World Cup stars away, we took a few of our young Academy players to gain experience with our A-League squad. Matt and I not going would save a few pennies on airfares and accommodation, and for me I could remain home to work with our new foreigner, the Brazilian Marco Tulio. He, like Jason, Moresche, Garang and Nectar, became one of my special projects.

In fact, all the boys at one time or another were special projects, either physically or mentally. Take Ballard, Nisbett and Steele, our diesel engines in the middle of the park. I would hound them every week until they embraced the more nasty side of midfield play! Even when we had won a match and they had played well, I would find a tackle, a header or anything they had missed or not engaged in and highlight that until it was fixed or they did it better.

THE VIBE MANAGER

Tulio reminded me of Silvera; they are two wonderfully talented, exquisite, top-level footballers. Artists and entertainers, they are the go-to guys in a team but I was more interested in their warrior characteristics because they had football quality in abundance. My job was to make them world-class athletes and teach them the art of war, both physically and mentally. Lucas Vilela, one of our first team and Academy Coaches, would help me, and together we had the Brazilian superstar ready for action in the second half of the season. He became one of our and the League's most valuable players. Moresche also remained with us, training by Tulio's side, and on Grand Final day he would score our sixth and final goal.

In Vanuatu, the boys played a series of games that were more like rugby league Test matches than football. No VAR and no rules proved a recipe for disaster, with good fortune our only ally. Brian, a beautiful soul, was welcomed and revered like a king returning home. For a man who only turned professional at 28, in his first season of A-League football he became pivotal for us. I recall Richard asking me at the start of our season who was our best central defender, at a time when we had not yet signed him and he was living off petty cash handouts from both Rich and Monty. I replied, "Brian."

Some in the Australian media labelled him a liability after his third send-off. They would all have to later eat their words. For my money, he was the best defender in the A-League all season, and capable of playing at much higher levels. Luckily for us, we managed to get the whole World Cup squad back to Australia injury-free, with match minutes under our belts, heat acclimatisation in our pockets, and having left every kid on the island nation with hope, joy and big smiles on their faces.

CHAPTER 8

PICTURES PAINT A THOUSAND WORDS

The visionary Richard Peil

In Canberra at pre-season training. L-R: Max Balard, Matt Simon, Dan Hall, Jason Cummings, me, Harrison Steele, Béni N'Kololo

With club legend Matt Simon

With Garang Kuol who at 17, played for the Socceroos at the 2022 World Cup (and wearing a great cap!)

With Jason Cummings

We were honoured to host the legendary, late Rale Rasic to Central Coast Stadium towards the end of the season before he was taken ill.

With my beautiful granddaughter, Zoe, at Sky Stadium, Wellington, New Zealand

Grand Final day – 1, the calm before the storm

With Nick 'Monty' Montgomery. This photo was taken and sent to Rale Rasic after our pre-match meal on Grand Final day. He was in intensive care.

Our special and powerful huddle this one away to Adelaide United in the semi-final first leg.

Celebrating the Grand Final win with captain Danny Vukovic holding the A-League trophy and club legendary supporter, Jake Banks, in front of the squad.

2023 A-League champions enjoying the vibe in the dressing room.

The traditional fans and family photo this one after securing our place in the 2023 A-League Grand Final.

CHAPTER 9

I'M THE JOKER

IT HAD JUST GONE MIDNIGHT. JAYNIE AND I STOOD AT THE top of the stairs, mingling with guests outside the ballroom of the Crowne Plaza Hotel in Terrigal. Most were heading home, and some to after-parties that had been preceded by an already eventful Mariners Medal Dinner.

Then we heard a loud bang at the bottom of the stairs that sounded like a car crash or small bomb going off. It had guests quickly heading for the hotel exits, including the man who had set off this commotion. Jason Cummings had just destroyed and demolished lighting, photographic and video equipment in the hotel foyer in a moment of madness that I somehow understood and, in a strange way, found funny.

Hotel staff rushed to the scene and one of them, obviously not a football fan, shouted out to Jason who was exiting the hotel, "Who are you, what's your name?" Jason stopped dead in his tracks, turned around and said, "I'm the Joker", before turning around again and heading off into the dark night!

This scene was a continuation of an already surreal night, one of the craziest I have witnessed. The star of the show was none other than Jason Cummings who, while collecting his top goal scorer trophy, would change character and become the Joker.

The Medal Dinner was for the most part the Josh Nisbett show, with the diminutive midfield powerhouse claiming award after award, including the Mariners Player of the Year. He would be joined by Newcomer of the Year, Nectar Triantis, and Coaches' Player of the Year, Brian Kaltak, but it would be the 'Joker' who would ultimately steal the show with one of the funniest award speeches I have ever witnessed.

In its own way, it was on a par with British comedian Ricky Gervais taking the piss out of Hollywood's elites whilst hosting the Golden Globes. Jason had been drinking all afternoon, worried about the speech he would have to deliver later that evening. How funny that a man so comfortable playing in front of millions around the world would find speaking to 30 tables in a ballroom so daunting, but this was not his comfort zone. To survive this ordeal, he decided he would have to change character and become the Joker!

Daniel McBreen, the former Mariners' striker and MC for the night, ran through Jason's goals and highlights for the season, then the Chairman's Award winner Matt Simon called Jason's name to receive a trophy, and that's where the fun began. Jason staggered haphazardly towards the microphone, as nervous as he was drunk.

Simmo handed him the trophy and the ballroom went silent. Everyone held their breath with anticipation, like the fans in the stadium when he would shoot on goal. Will it go in, will it not? Only this time there was no ball, no football pitch, just Jason staring into what must have seemed like a dark hell. You could hear a pin drop as he moved the microphone to his mouth and said, "How you going?", in the most perfect Australian accent ever.

I suppose it was his way of breaking the ice, but all it did was send a nervous shiver into all of us sitting there. He rattled off a couple of teammates' names, as Danny Vukovic had told him to do, but you could tell he wasn't himself anymore. He was a completely different man, not the Jason we all loved. The shit was about to hit the proverbial fan as he steadied himself and began to focus on me, sitting at the Chairman's table a few yards in front of him. He said, "My mate Andy Bernal deserves an award", or words to that effect, immediately followed by a monologue that spared no topic or nobody. It was a concoction of words more powerful and shocking than the concoction of drinks he had already consumed and one that would have had him sacked immediately by any other club.

The whole ballroom sat in shock, except for Banksy, one of our greatest supporters, who was in raptures of laughter. Many of Jason's teammates had slumped into their chairs, not believing what they were hearing. To this day I have no idea why he said what he said. Maybe my cocaine stories and supermodel parties at Ronaldo Nazário's house had locked themselves into his psyche somewhere, into his subconscious mind. Maybe he was directing it at me as a cry for help and wanting to be saved in some way; I'll never know. I don't think he'll ever know, but what I do know is Ronaldo, the Brazilian one, would love Jason. They would be the perfect golf and party mates.

Simmo escorted him off the stage. He was not in a good state of mind, and was now not our much-loved number nine, not the world-class sharp-shooter anymore, he had turned into a stranger, an uncontrollable villain. The table next to mine which had several local and NSW government officials at it sat in silence, stone-faced, a few of them with their mouths open like codfish, probably trying to decipher what they had just heard. One of their wives tapped me on the shoulder and asked me, "Did he just say what I heard him say?" I said, "Yes, ma'am, you heard correctly."

Fast forward a short while, and the Joker was now totally out of control.

Like Elvis, he had left the building, and was now jumping on car roofs as if they were trampolines. He then decided to take a run up and launch himself like Superman at a parked car, trying to fly through the windscreen. A loud thud resonated around the street as he hit the windscreen face first with his body dropping to the ground like a sack of potatoes. Rebounding immediately to his feet, he continued his mad assault on anything and everything. Many of his young teammates were worried; they'd never witnessed this level of madness before.

At this point, I parked the club's A-League Isuzu Ute in the middle of the road between the hotel and Rhonda's nightclub, jumped out with Jaynie, and like Batman and Robin, we gave chase, but it was futile. Like a jungle cat, he was proving to be elusive and without a tranquilliser gun, it was an almost impossible mission. I can only imagine explaining all this action to the local police who were stationed 50 metres away, just around the corner, but fortunately for all of us they saw or heard nothing!

Monty, his wife, Josie, and Jason's teammate Steeley (his guardian angel) finally found him in his apartment where they somehow calmed him down with a cup of English breakfast tea, but the Joker wasn't finished. He was playing possum with them, and as soon as they all left, he returned to the night once again, this time around 5 a.m., completely naked (other than a Hanna G-string) and wanting to fight the world.

He would again disappear into the dark of night. We had lost him. He was missing in action, and try as we might, we heard nothing and had no contact. The following day, Monty had me driving around Terrigal looking for him. His residence and phone were as silent as the night he had disappeared into. Steeley finally got a hold of him late that afternoon and not long after I received the following text message from Jason, "I'm all good brother, mad night for sure, it was a classic. Appreciate your message, love you and never forget the world needs bad guys like us"!

I could write a whole book on Jason and his mad adventures, but I'll leave it to him to tell the world his entire life story one day. Like my story, his is like a movie too. His party-bus antics on Mad Monday will go down as one of the funniest things I've ever seen in my whole life.

I'm honoured and grateful to have worked with him individually as I previously did with David Beckham, Tim Cahill and Tom Rogic. This ride with Jason was a different one though. It contained no agent or management bullshit. This was purely friendship, football, boxing, athletic development, fun and laughter, and lots of it. He is a crazy genius, like Maradona and Gascoigne; it's a fine line, as they say. Well, he lives on that line. He's loved by adoring fans, adored by all his teammates, misunderstood by some, a beautiful soul, a free spirit and the best friend you could ever wish for. He was my own Vibe Manager in the 2022–23 A-League season.

CHAPTER 10

AFTERMATH

WITH THE MARINERS MEDAL NIGHT DONE AND DUSTED, we now had to focus on our upcoming game away to Adelaide United in 10 days' time. There were calls by many to punish Jason, to sack him, to bench him, to drop him, but that wasn't how Monty worked. Good people, and Jason is one, we could fix. Rather than ignore him, punish him and toss him out, we nursed him, fixed him and reset him within days.

In the lead-up to the match, Monty put up the progressively changing photo of the 2013 Championship-winning team, as he had been doing throughout the season. After every win, he would have a player or staff head on the 10-year-old photo replaced by one of ours. It was manifestation at its most artistic level. The only head not to be replaced was that of Monty himself, who was part of the 2013 team and still with us.

As we won games, the picture changed, and with one final game of the season remaining, only one other head remained from the 2013 team. It belonged to the captain and club legend John Hutchinson, and Monty had chosen my head to replace John's if we beat Adelaide in the final game! What an honour to bestow on someone. Ezio told me not long ago that Monty reserved that spot for me as a tribute. It was a gesture that I don't really have enough words of gratitude for, but it meant the world to me. The championship-winning puzzle awaited its final piece. The reality was that we could not afford to lose another single match, as it would ruin not only the photo but our season. No pressure, as they say.

Off we went to Adelaide, a beautiful city with a beautiful football stadium, and in front of a full house we played our trump card, the Joker. In the warm-up, the young kid the whole nation was talking about, Nestory Irankunda, tried what all the opposing teams' Goalkeeper Coaches had tried all season, and again I was having none of it. While we warmed up in our half, and they warmed up in their own, the kid decided he would come into our half and put on a juggling show for his adoring home fans. Why? I have no idea; he should have been with Adelaide's other substitutes.

Seconds later and after a word in his ear, off he trotted back into his half, never to return. Lesson learnt, and he would not return for his warm-up stunt in either of the two following semi-final legs. The wonderkid that global agents and teams had come to watch would be extinguished by one of our wonderkids, Jacob Farrell, and English club Sunderland FC who had come to watch him play would instead choose another wonderkid, our very own Nectar Triantis. We had plenty of them!

We destroyed them 4–1 in one of our best performances of the season, and in doing so, we clinched second spot and AFC (Asian Football Confederation) Cup qualification. There is nothing sweeter than doing it in your opponents' backyard. While sitting in the changeroom, savouring a wonderful victory, Jason told me, "That was for Candy Montgomery", words that stemmed from an exercise Ezio had given the team before the match in honour of Monty's mum who had passed away a few years earlier.

Jason knew how much Monty loved him, and how much he'd done for him from day one. He had backed him big time since the drama of Medal night, so he planned to repay 'the gaffer' with his heart, soul and goals, and plenty of them in the coming weeks. We left the away dressing room spotless as usual; the Japanese national team would have been proud of us. It was just what we did, being respectful on and off the pitch, both in victory and defeat. On the way back to the hotel in Adelaide, Jason texted me from the back of the bus, "I used to think my life was a tragedy, now I realise it's a comedy." The Joker certainly had the last laugh!

THE VIBE MANAGER

We would now face Adelaide United again in a two-legged semi-final, away first then at home for the second leg. Like the 4–1 drubbing a week earlier, Adelaide was a happy hunting ground for me. The last match I played there was against Adelaide City, marking Carl Veart who was now the Adelaide United Coach. We won 1–0 and I was lucky enough to score the winner that day, so bring on the city of churches, it held no fear.

Adelaide's captain and most important player, Craig Goodwin, after scoring a goal in the World Cup, had appointed himself the voice of global football knowledge. He began telling the world's football media how we played, and how they would defeat us. Apparently, we were now a long ball team! Bottom line, he was wrong on all counts and should have focused more on trying to get out of Storm Roux's back pocket rather than opining on things he knew nothing about.

Over the next two matches, we continued our season-long domination of the Reds. We won the first leg in Adelaide 2–1, following exactly the same processes over and over. For them, tactical changes were fruitless, because we just did us, as we always did. We changed for nobody; we were always trying to win and win well. We were now set up nicely for the second leg in front of a capacity crowd of 20,059 at Industree Group Stadium at home on the Central Coast.

THE VIBE MANAGER

The thought of slipping up crossed the mind occasionally, that nightmare scenario you never want to come true, but our minds were far more positively balanced. This team was on a roll and there would be no stopping us. We had mentally got to a level where pressure was our friend. We loved it, we desired it. Our opponents, however, would succumb to it and crumble, 2–0 on the night, 4–1 on aggregate. To add to the night's entertainment, I tackled a pitch invader headed for Jason. It was a bit like English wicketkeeper Jonny Bairstow's effort at Lord's in the 2023 Ashes series, but I added a judo throw before securing him in a headlock. Nobody was touching my man with the Grand Final just around the corner.

CHAPTER 11

THE BIG DANCE

PARRAMATTA-BOUND, WE BOARDED THE TEAM BUS AFTER our Thursday morning training session for a beautiful lunch put on by Chef Dan at the COE. Many years ago, I had lost and then won a Grand Final at Parramatta Stadium, now the more modern CommBank Stadium, and I couldn't help wondering what my third Grand Final visit would bring. Only time would tell, but first the boys would have to attend the annual A-League awards two nights before the big match against Melbourne City.

As expected, and as per our football season so far, we were given nothing and won nothing! For me, we certainly deserved some accolades, in particular Tulio's goal which should have been Goal of the Season, and Monty should have been named Coach of the Year.

Instead, Coach of the Year went to Adelaide United's Carl Veart, whose team we had dismantled and demolished over three games prior to the

Grand Final with the total aggregate score 8–2! In a most insane and stupid ruling, the best coach in the country in the A-League could only sit at the awards and watch the second-best coach pick up the prize. Monty was ineligible because of a red card he received in a match earlier in the season against Wellington Phoenix.

Veart's win was embarrassing for the A-League, I presume, when all the world and everybody in the country knew it belonged to the Mariners' Head Coach. Carl Veart knew it too, but never look a gift horse in the mouth, as they say, so up he went and collected his prize. What I would have done, and what he should have done, was go up, accept the award and then hand it to Nick Montgomery, the former captain and legend of Sheffield United, the team Carl had spent a few seasons playing up front for. Now that would have been the ultimate act of humility and respect.

But it didn't faze our leader one bit. Maybe he was a little disappointed, but he had the kind words and backing of many top-flight managers in the English premiership who had congratulated him on the season so far and were wishing him all the best for the Grand Final. Their words meant more to him than any individual accolade, and missing out only spurred him on. It gave him more fuel for a fire that we would light, fight, control and exterminate a few days later at CommBank Stadium.

THE VIBE MANAGER

With the awards night done and dusted, the boys settled into their normal routines at the Parramatta Holiday Inn. The famous Holiday Inn wasn't the Coogee Crowne Plaza or any other Sydney-based Crowne Plaza that the A-Leagues would have for us to stay in, but it was more 'us', more community, more modest and more family. It was the perfect fit and five minutes on the bus from CommBank Stadium.

But for me it brought back two horrible memories. The Holiday Inn was the hotel we returned to in Reading, England, after losing our Wembley play-off final. It was also the same hotel I ran to when trying to escape the Thames Valley Police force. Only a win could erase these previous two nightmares that often still haunted my brain over the years. Surely, it would be third time lucky!

We prepared the same, nothing changed. Ezio's usual signs carrying inspirational messages were strategically placed around the dining and team room, but truth be told, the mood was nice, relaxed and quietly confident. An Ezio masterstroke was the only addition and it would prove to be empowering. It was a large picture of the statue of David wearing a Mariners' shirt and it greeted us upon entry to our team dining room — a constant reminder that another Goliath was soon to be slayed!

The vibe was good, so good that even the opponent's non-playing captain,

THE VIBE MANAGER

Scott Jamieson, made reference to it days before the match on the *A-Leagues All Access* show. His words "They have their Vibe Manager and we have our players" would not age well, and despite myself taking it as a feather in my cap and an increase in my personal stock, it was disrespectful to our club, fans, coaching staff and especially our players. They were fuming, and rather than rattle them, it gave them even more power.

A journalist also led Jamieson down the Bambi path, insinuating that the minor premiers would be the alpha males in the contest and we were more like Bambi. Again, his words in response would not age well. He stated, "If we have to take down Bambi, so be it. I could not care less." It was a lot of disrespectful talk from a player who was retiring from football after this match, and who had played very little minutes all season. On the Saturday night of the Grand Final, we planned to give 'Jamo' a retirement send-off that he would never forget. It turned out to be one that even we could never have imagined in one of the greatest football matches ever witnessed in Australia.

Our fuel levels were stacked, as weeks earlier Melbourne City Coach Rado Vidosic said that he believed they would be playing Adelaide United in the final! They were unbelievable words from a coach who had never won a men's Grand Final, only winning the Premier's Plate on the back of inheriting Patrick Kisnorbo's wonderful team. We had demolished Adelaide in the past few weeks and his comments showed total disrespect to arguably the most in-form football team in the competition. Was he even watching us play?

The last time we played Melbourne City, I had gone to shake his hand after the match and he blanked me, so he had it coming too. Win, lose or draw, I was always brought up to shake my opponents' hands; it's respect. Six of the best goals had him pathetically apologising to his Director of Football after the match, and quickly realising that the men's and women's football (he'd had some success in the latter) were two very different animals.

There was even more fuel to come. If we lit all of it, we would have had to call the NSW Fire Brigade! I couldn't believe it, this time it was from a friend, Ernie Merrick, Football Australia's Chief Football Officer. The 'top dog' wrote on the Keep Up social media platform, "Whenever I have been involved in a Grand Final, I always sought to base my team around the holy trinity of experience, goal scorers and a reliable goalkeeper."

On the latter two, Ernie was spot on, as our starting line-up had plenty of goal scorers in Cummings, N'Kololo, Silvera and Tulio, along with the A-League's best and most experienced goalkeeper, Danny Vukovic. At this point, he was going great guns and should have stopped, but he didn't, adding "Melbourne City will win" and "The sad reality of real life is that fairy tales rarely come true".

It seemed the whole world was against us, but we had manifested our situation. I could feel it, we believed and we would conquer. The day of the game Monty, myself, Simmo and Ezio caught up for a morning coffee with Chairman Richard. It was another calm morning, another day at the office, and more coffee with Ezio, just to set up the day in the Mariners' normal orderly fashion. That afternoon, a few bizarre and strange occurrences, and one sad one would give us even more empowerment. The coaching staff decided to do a gym session prior to our pre- match meal, nothing too spectacular but a nice calmer before the evening that lay ahead.

Speaking of gyms, we were in the final stages of finishing our own one at the COE. Richard had bought all the equipment, but it remained in boxes the whole season. Delayed planning permission had forced us into eventually building the gym from donated shipping containers and structural domes from China that came with either no instructions or Chinese instructions (as did the saunas and ice baths!).

Matt Simon and Richard's nephew Josh Hegarty would somehow put these monstrosities together, well into the early hours of the morning, aided sometimes by Richard, Dobbo, Monty and myself. Where else in the world would you have the Sporting Director, Chairman, Team Manager and Coaches working on a club building site!

Can you believe we created human machines in a gym that was no more than an alleyway between our training sheds and the Tuggerah Soccer 5s football business? Like the backstreets of Sydney, London or New York, we at times shared the alleyway with the local mice and rats that inhabited the area, but the boys never complained once. Our old, rustic weights and kettlebells, weathered mats, decade-old ropes and bands were a million miles away from Melbourne City's world-class training equipment and facilities, but for all of us, a chin-up bar was a chin-up bar, irrespective of its location.

But back to our pre-match gym session. We set an exercise time while the hotel gym's MTV channel played some golden oldies. As we exited, 'We Are the Champions' by Queen came on. We couldn't believe it, but we all felt it was a sign from somewhere that it would be our night.

As if that wasn't prophetic enough, while having our pre-match meal I received a text from my good friend Jack Zervos, who was with our mutual friend, legendary Socceroos Coach, Rale Rasic, who unfortunately only had days to live. Rale had come to watch us play against Sydney FC months earlier and loved what Monty was doing. The message from Jack read, "Rale sends his love and best wishes from his hospital bed to you, Monty and the team."

I replied with a photo of Monty and myself, and a blue and yellow love heart. Rale's last words to Jack that day were, "Andy, he's a good man, incredible character, so brave. Monty, Monty he's a 'Blade' [nickname given to Sheffield United] you know, one of their best, what a great team. 15 years a 'Blade', but do the fans in Australia really know what this means? I doubt it. These men are royalty, both of these men are what football is all about. Tell them I send my love and respect."

Leaving the hotel, I ran into former Socceroo teammate Milan Ivanovic, who I hadn't seen for 30 years or so. He was there to present the Joe Marston Medal to the most valuable player on the pitch (or 'best on ground' as it's sometimes referred to), the very medal he had won back in the day. Abbas Saad, our Mariners Academy Head Coach, was the first recipient of this prestigious honour when we won the 1990 Grand Final, so when Milan told me he was hoping to present it to a Central Coast Mariners' player, I felt that somehow the football gods were all coming together, wanting us to win.

The warm-up was interesting, to say the least. The last time we had met, their Goalkeeper Coach thought it would be a good idea to have his keeper deliver long balls over the halfway line into drills that our players were doing.

After a couple of warnings and respectfully asking him not to do this, he continued. The final long ball went over my head and into our 18-yard box. He turned and sprinted to the ball, picked it up and began running back into his own half. At that very moment, I decided the Dutchman needed to be 'welcomed to country' and taught a little football respect, so I lined him up, and with a State of Origin shoulder charge, nailed him, ball and all!

Off he whimpered to the bench where he relayed what had happened to the rest of the coaching staff. They all looked over at me, saying and doing nothing. To be honest, for a split second I had thought of leaving my elbow a little higher and knocking his teeth out, but with my past record, the A-League would have probably banned me for life, so on this occasion the Keeper Coach got 'nice Andy'!

You would think they would have learnt from that incident, but no. This time, the Keeper Coach sent their young number two keeper, not himself, into the fire. As Tommy Glover launched his first long ball 15 metres into our half, I dropped a little hip and shoulder into him with the words "Fuck off back into your own half."

Scott Jamieson saw this and walked towards the halfway line, shouting, "Don't fucking touch him, he's a kid." He had a microphone on him, so it was his moment to talk tough, at one point calling me a "knob head".

THE VIBE MANAGER

Of all the things he could have called me, he called me a knob head!

Talk is cheap though; I didn't give a shit what he called me, and I didn't give a shit if the keeper was a kid, if it was Jamieson himself, or their whole team. If they were in our half, they would be removed. I actually found it amusing, but my intervention ended their long-ball drills and I was now really in their heads.

To be honest, there was nothing in it, and if Scott Jamieson had really wanted some action, he would have walked over the halfway line and gone for me. It would have made my day, but it was never going to happen. Stamati and Sergio were never going to let me get near him and it's a heat 'Jamo' didn't need. Anyway, more importantly, we had a football match to win in front of our thousands of adoring fans.

The game kicked off and we were on fire, with Jason putting us 1–0 up early, then not long after Sammy 'the prince' Silvera would double our lead, only to concede a goal not long before half-time that got City back into the match. In all honesty, the game should have been all over by then as we had carved them up with some beautiful football. Tulio, Cummings and N'Kololo all had great chances denied by Glover, who despite conceding six goals for the match, was arguably their best player on the day. That in itself told a story!

THE VIBE MANAGER

Half-time came and Monty gave his usual eloquent and empowering talk, but we commenced the second half slowly and City began to take charge of proceedings. Sunderland-bound Nectar Triantis kept us in the game, clearing a ball that got past Vukovic and was heading towards goal, then suddenly a special moment in time changed the tempo.

Super-sub Jacob 'Faz' Farrell came on, and before you knew it, he had won two penalties for us that Jason converted with perfect precision, giving the 'Cumdog Millionaire' (as commentator Simon Hill described him) his Grand Final hat-trick, a very special moment indeed. It was now 4–1 and it seemed like time was flying, as fast as the two goals that were about to come. The first from Frenchman Benny N'Kololo, and the final nail in the coffin from Brazilian, Moresche.

With not much time left on the clock, Matt Simon and I couldn't believe it when we saw City's captain Scott Jamieson refuse to come on, presumably not wanting to be in any way associated with this 6–1 humiliation. There was no more talk, the *Titanic* had sunk and its captain had abandoned ship. We had sunk them in 90 minutes in one of the greatest games ever seen in this country. The youngest team in the competition had disabled, dismantled and destroyed a club owned by one of the wealthiest and most powerful organisations on the planet (City Football Group).

The final whistle went and approximately 25,000 Mariners' fans went wild; for many it was the greatest day of their lives. Jaynie went nuts, so did her mum, Eileen, along with other friends in the Chairman's box that included Liverpool FC legend Craig Johnston and Australian cricket legend Steve Waugh. On the pitch celebrating with all the players and staff as our captain Danny Vukovic lifted the trophy, it was possibly one of the greatest days of my life too. How on earth did I get here? That was the million-dollar question.

We had silenced many doubters, but for Monty and me, Melbourne City had held no fear. Respect always, but no fear. We had both played against Manchester City in England and this lot, despite the arrogance they carried themselves with and the colours they played in, were not the calibre of Manchester City squads, and definitely were not Pep Guardiola's magnificent men. They were an inferior model, put together by their owners to conquer Australia and continue building the City Group brand's global presence. There's nothing wrong with that, only that someone forgot to tell their coaches and players.

They had underestimated the form team. We were a truly magnificent team who had demolished all previous records set by our club's 2013 Grand Final-winning team, who 10 years earlier had a bigger playing budget than our newly crowned heroes! It was simply extraordinary for a club who almost went bankrupt, saw Graham Arnold depart for Japan, and was saved only by English businessman Mike Charlesworth who took full control with a mission to keep the Mariners alive.

It was now time to celebrate back at the Holiday Inn. I had now erased all my previous negativity linked to the world-famous hotel chain, in the process becoming one of the few people to win the Grand Final as a player and now in a coaching capacity as one of Nick Montgomery's lieutenants. I called Mum straight after the final and she was in tears. Her first words were, "Your father would have been so proud of you."

The after-party continued long into the night and long into the next day with our final destination being Drifter's Wharf Bar for a private players and family function. It was a function that embodied the madness and craziness of who we were as a team, as a group, and a function that would end with Chairman Richard Peil, Jason Cummings and Harry Steele engaged in a three-way 'Wrestlemania' that went on for 30 minutes and achieved absolutely nothing besides hilariously entertaining those in attendance and leaving the place looking like it had been hit by a bar-room brawl.

Rich (a judo black belt) was in his element, the other two were winging it with their very own UFC moves and Steeley producing the highlight of the night. It was a judo throw (and a very good one) on Liam Chauncy, an innocent and unsuspecting bystander who went flying into the night and got up feeling like it was tomorrow!

Before this mania that was a part of how we rolled, there was a poignant moment I could never have imagined growing up in white, racist Canberra and it was a highlight of our arrival at Drifter's for our private function. The timing coincided with the end of the NRL rugby league clash between the Canterbury Bulldogs and the Sydney Roosters. As 20,000 fans exited Industree Group Stadium, the Mariners' team bus approached the roundabout adjacent to the palm trees that line the ocean end of the stadium. Fans on their way home began shouting and clapping, lining both sides of the main thoroughfare in and out of Gosford, creating what seemed like a never-ending guard of honour. Once parked, the bus was immediately surrounded by thousands of rugby league fans wanting selfies, autographs and to touch the A-League champions!

For me, that moment signified how far we have come as a nation and how football (or soccer or whatever you want to call it) has changed and impacted the landscape of Australian sport. In my childhood, if you played football, you were called a sheila, wog or a poofter and I was often called all three. My friend and Socceroos' legend Johnny Warren titled his autobiography those exact three words so to now have the admiration, respect and love from a rival code and its supporters was a special moment in time. It felt like our win the night before had further transcended football in this country and that it had in a magical way embedded itself deeper into the very fabric of our society.

In the end, the 2022–23 was a very special A-League season and an amazing ride that proved fairy tales do come true. One may happen again or it may not, but history will remember this one well. Once again, as with the first chapter of my life, I had proven many doubters wrong because impossible means nothing for the *Original Wizard of Oz*.

SPECIAL MENTIONS

 I WANT ESPECIALLY TO ACKNOWLEDGE TWO PEOPLE WITH Central Coast Mariners who deserve recognition for what they have done for the club, and who have also been a good friend to me.

Shaun Mielekamp: Shaun commenced in the role of CEO in 2015 and has endured more dark days than glory days at the club so this Grand Final was a special one for him—a testament to his hard work, resilience and perseverance. It brought him to tears and I'm glad I played a little role in helping him and the club achieve another Championship. My wife Jaynie works as his PA and we are both very grateful for his support, kindness and friendship.

Anton Tagliaferro: Anton is a hugely successful businessman and a great guy who for many years now has helped fund the club's scholarship program including providing many Academy players with accommodation.

THE VIBE MANAGER

He is hugely respected by all the players and coaching staff. He travels with the team regularly and the young ones are lucky to experience financial wisdom from one of the best on the planet. Sammy Silvera and Garang Kuol are two wonderful examples of Anton's generosity.

I know I speak for everyone at the club when I say thank you Anton for your ongoing support.

ABOUT

ANDY BERNAL

ONE OF THE PIONEERS FOR AUSTRALIAN FOOTBALLERS abroad, Andy Bernal is the son of Spanish migrants and grew up in Canberra. Andy's love of football, although second to rugby league as a child, saw him emerge from the ACT to forge a career abroad, becoming a professional in both Spain and England.

In between times, Andy had a spell back home, winning a National Championship with Sydney Olympic FC and gaining Socceroos selection. He became an integral part of one of the greatest teams in the history of Reading FC, being considered by many supporters as one of their greatest ever talents.

After his retirement, Andy became a football agent and was entrusted to be Manager in Spain to superstar David Beckham following his move to Real Madrid from Manchester United.

Following roles as a Socceroos scout and a Strength and Conditioning Coach, he is now Head of Athletic Development and 'Vibe Manager' at Central Coast Mariners Football Club.

He is married to Jaynie Wignall, a proud father to Isabella who married UFC star Dan Hooker, and as well as a proud grandfather to Zoe. Andy lives on the Central Coast of NSW.

His autobiography *Riding Shotgun – the Autobiography of the Original Wizard of Oz* was published by Fair Play Publishing in 2021.

APPENDIX

CENTRAL COAST MARINERS THE ROAD TO THE 2023 A-LEAGUE MEN CHAMPIONSHIP

COMPILED BY
ANDREW HOWE

THE VIBE MANAGER

Season Home and Away		Result		Goalscorers / Time Scored	Position
Wellington Phoenix	(A)	D	2–2	Silvera 60, Cummings 65	8th
Perth Glory	(H)	L	1–2	Silvera 21	11th
Western United	(H)	W	4–2	Cummings 67, N'Kololo 73, Farrell 78, Ayongo 88	6th
Western Sydney Wanderers	(A)	W	3–0	Ruhs 66, 72, Silvera 81	3rd
Macarthur FC	(H)	L	2–3	Kuol 65 pen, 72	5th
Newcastle Jets	(H)	L	1–2	Cummings 53	8th
Sydney FC	(H)	W	2–1	Marco Tulio 36, Hall 39	4th
Newcastle Jets	(H)	W	3–0	Marco Tulio 22, Cummings 65, N'Kololo 87 pen	3rd
Melbourne City	(A)	L	0–1		4th
Melbourne Victory	(H)	W	2–1	Cummings 11, 53	2nd
Adelaide United	(H)	W	4–0	Own goal 31, 55, N'Kololo 48, Farrell 58	2nd
Macarthur FC	(A)	W	2–1	Marco Tulio 4, Cummings 26	2nd
Wellington Phoenix	(A)	L	1–2	N'Kololo 93	2nd
Western Sydney Wanderers	(H)	D	2–2	Silvera 30, Cummings 72	2nd
Sydney FC	(A)	L	2–3	Cummings 20 pen, 33	2nd
Brisbane Roar	(A)	W	2–1	Marco Tulio 19, N'Kololo 70 pen	2nd
Perth Glory	(A)	D	2–2	Cummings 74 pen, 81 pen	2nd
Wellington Phoenix	(H)	D	1–1	McGarry 12	2nd
Western Sydney Wanderers	(A)	L	0–2		4th
Macarthur FC	(H)	W	4–1	McGarry 31, Cummings 47, 63 pen, Marco Tulio 51	3rd
Melbourne Victory	(A)	L	0–2		4th
Brisbane Roar	(H)	W	4–1	Marco Tulio 15, Nisbet 17, Own goal 30, Cummings 58 pen	3rd
Western United	(A)	W	3–0	Cummings 21, N'Kololo 35, Wenzel-Halls 91	3rd
Melbourne City	(H)	D	1–1	Nisbet 78	3rd
Newcastle Jets	(A)	W	3–1	Silvera 28, 58, Marco Tulio 69	2nd
Adelaide United	(A)	W	4–1	Marco Tulio 23, 57, N'Kololo 42, Steele 87	2nd

Semi-Final Home and Away	Result	Goalscorers / Time Scored
Adelaide United (A)	W 2–1	**McGarry** 15, **Cummings** 37
Adelaide United (H)	W 2–0	**Silvera** 48, **Marco Tulio** 52
Central Coast Mariners win 4–1 on aggregate and progress to the Grand Final		

Grand Final	Result	Goalscorers / Time Scored
Melbourne City	W 6–1	**Cummings** 21, 65 pen, 73 pen, **Silvera** 34, **N'Kololo** 83, **Moresche** 91

Grand Final details

Central Coast Mariners line-up:

Danny Vukovic (c), **Storm Roux** *(Dan Hall 78')*, **Nectarios Triantis** *(Moresche 85')*, **Brian Kaltak**, **Max Balard** *(Harrison Steele 78')*, **Josh Nisbet**, **Béni N'Kololo**, **James McGarry** *(Jacob Farrell 63')*, **Samuel Silvera** *(Christian Theoharous 85')*, **Jason Cummings**, **Marco Tulio**

Date Played
3 June 2023

Venue
CommBank Stadium, Sydney

Referee
Chris Beath

Attendance
26,523

Season appearances/goals

Marco Tulio (29/10)
Samuel Silvera (29/8)
Danny Vukovic (29/0)
Jason Cummings (28/20)
Josh Nisbet (28/2)
Max Balard (26/0)
Béni N'Kololo (26/8)
Storm Roux (26/0)
Jacob Farrell (25/2)
Brian Kaltak (25/0)
Nectarios Triantis (25/0)
Harrison Steele (24/1)
Dan Hall (19/1)
Christian Theoharous (17/0)
Michael Ruhs (15/2)
James McGarry (14/3),
Thomas Aquilina (12/0)
Matheus Moresche (11/1)
Paul Ayongo (9/1)
Garang Kuol (9/2)
Sasha Kuzevski (8/0)
Cameron Windust (7/0)
James Bayliss (6/0)
Kelechi John (3/0)
Dylan Wenzel-Halls (3/1)
Nicholas Duarte (2/0)
Dor Jok (2/0)
Miguel Di Pizio (1/0)
Yinka Sunmola (1/0)
Zac Zoricich (1/0)

Head coaches

Nick Montgomery (28 games)

Sergio Raimundo (1 game)

MORE REALLY GOOD
FOOTBALL BOOKS FROM
FAIR PLAY PUBLISHING

fairplaypublishing.com.au/shop

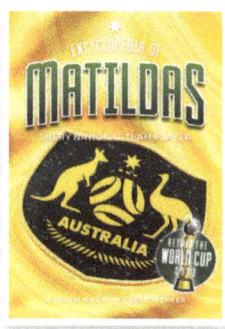
Encyclopedia of Matildas
Beyond the World Cup 2023

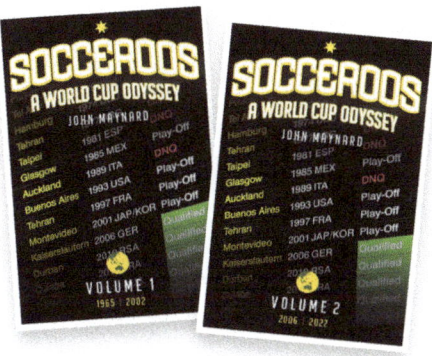
Socceroos – A World Cup Odyssey,
1965 to 2022 Volumes 1 and 2

Football Fans
In Their Own Write

"Get Your Tits Out
for the Lads"

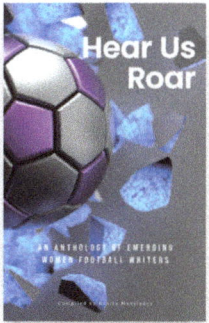
Hear Us Roar
– An anthology of
emerging women
football writers

When Mum and Dad
See Me Kick

Noddy
– The Untold Story of
Adrian Alston

www.ingramcontent.com/pod-product-compliance
Lightning Source LLC
Chambersburg PA
CBHW051316110526
44590CB00031B/4372